Vamos a contar / Counting Books

Comer pares
Contar frutas y vegetales de dos en dos

Eating Pairs
Counting Fruits and Vegetables by Two

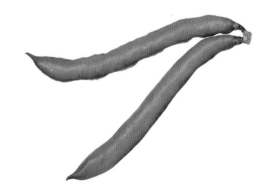

por/by Sarah L. Schuette

Consultora/Consultant:
Joan Bushman, MPH, RD
American Dietetic Association

CAPSTONE PRESS
a capstone imprint

A+ Books are published by Capstone Press
1710 Roe Crest Drive, North Mankato, Minnesota 56003.
www.capstonepub.com

Books published by Capstone Press are manufactured with paper containing at least 10 percent post-consumer waste.

Library of Congress Cataloging-in-Publication Data
Schuette, Sarah L., 1976–
 [Eating pairs. Spanish & English]
 Comer pares = Eating pairs : contar frutas y vegetales de dos en dos/counting fruits and vegetables by two / por/by Sarah L. Schuette.
      p. cm.—(Vamos a contar = Counting books)
 Includes index.
 Summary: "From two heads of cabbage to twenty tomatoes, provides simple facts about fruits and vegetables as their numbers increase by twos, until one hundred peas appear to be counted—in both English and Spanish"—Provided by publisher.
  ISBN 978-1-4296-8251-0 (library binding)
 1. Counting—Juvenile literature. 2. Multiplication—Juvenile literature. 3. Fruit—Juvenile literature.
4. Vegetables—Juvenile literature. I. Title.
 QA113.S388818 2012
 513.2'11—dc23   2011028679

Credits

Strictly Spanish, translation services; Heather Kindseth, designer; Eric Manske, bilingual book designer; Deirdre Barton, media researcher; Laura Manthe, production specialist

Photo Credits

Artville, beans, mushrooms, pears, potatoes
Capstone Press/Gary Sundermeyer, cover
PhotoDisc, Inc., apples, bananas, cabbages, peaches, peas, raspberries, tomatoes

Note to Parents, Teachers, and Librarians

Comer pares/Eating Pairs uses color photographs and a nonfiction format to introduce children to fruits and vegetables while building mastery of basic counting skills in both English and Spanish. It is designed to be read aloud to a pre-reader or to be read independently by an early reader. The images help early readers and listeners understand the text and concepts discussed. The book encourages further learning by including the following sections: Glossary, Internet Sites, and Index. Early readers may need assistance using these features.

Printed in the United States of America in North Mankato, Minnesota.
102011   006405CGS12

3

2

Cabbage heads are crinkly, green vegetables. On St. Patrick's Day, many people cook corned beef with cabbage for dinner.

———————————————

Las cabezas de repollo son vegetales verdes y arrugados. En el Día de San Patricio, mucha gente cocina *corned beef* con repollo para la cena.

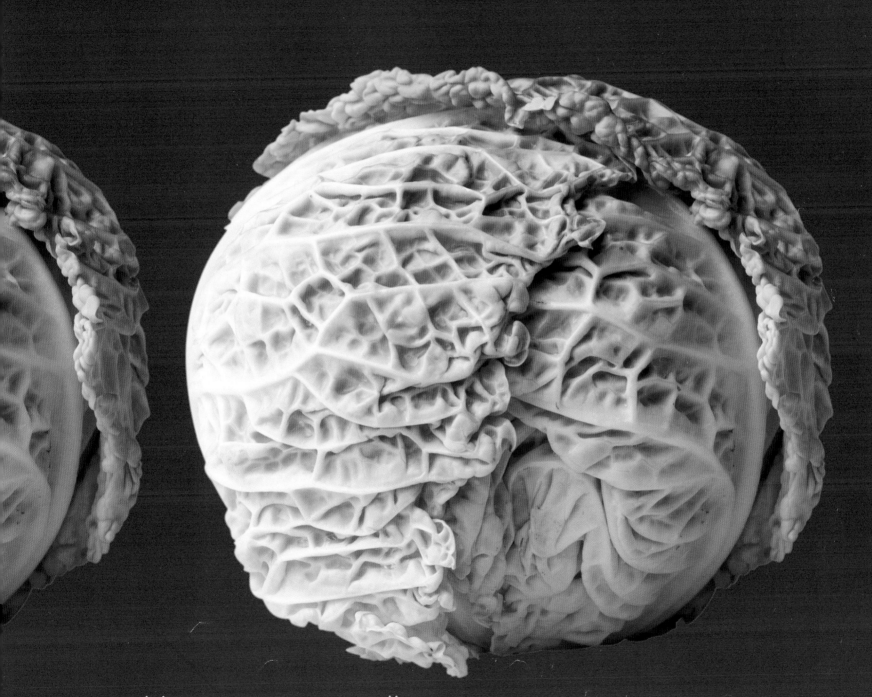

Two cabbages / Dos repollos

Apples have small seeds inside. The apple seeds can be planted for a new apple tree to grow.

Las manzanas tienen pequeñas semillas adentro. Las semillas de la manzana pueden plantarse para que crezca un manzano nuevo.

Four apples / Cuatro manzanas

6

Banana skins are easy to peel.
Many people eat breakfast cereal
with banana slices on top.

Six bananas /
Seis bananas

Las cáscaras de banana son fáciles de pelar. Mucha gente desayuna cereal con rodajas de banana por encima.

2
4
6
8
10
12
14
16
18
20
100

8

Eight pears /
Ocho peras

Pears are related to apples and are part of the rose family. All types of pears are juicy and sweet.

———————————————

Las peras son parientes de las manzanas y pertenecen a la familia de la rosa. Todas las clases de peras son jugosas y dulces.

10

Potatoes are tubers and grow underground. People eat potatoes mashed, boiled, baked, and as French fries.

_____

Las papas son tubérculos y crecen bajo tierra. La gente come papas en puré, hervidas, horneadas y fritas.

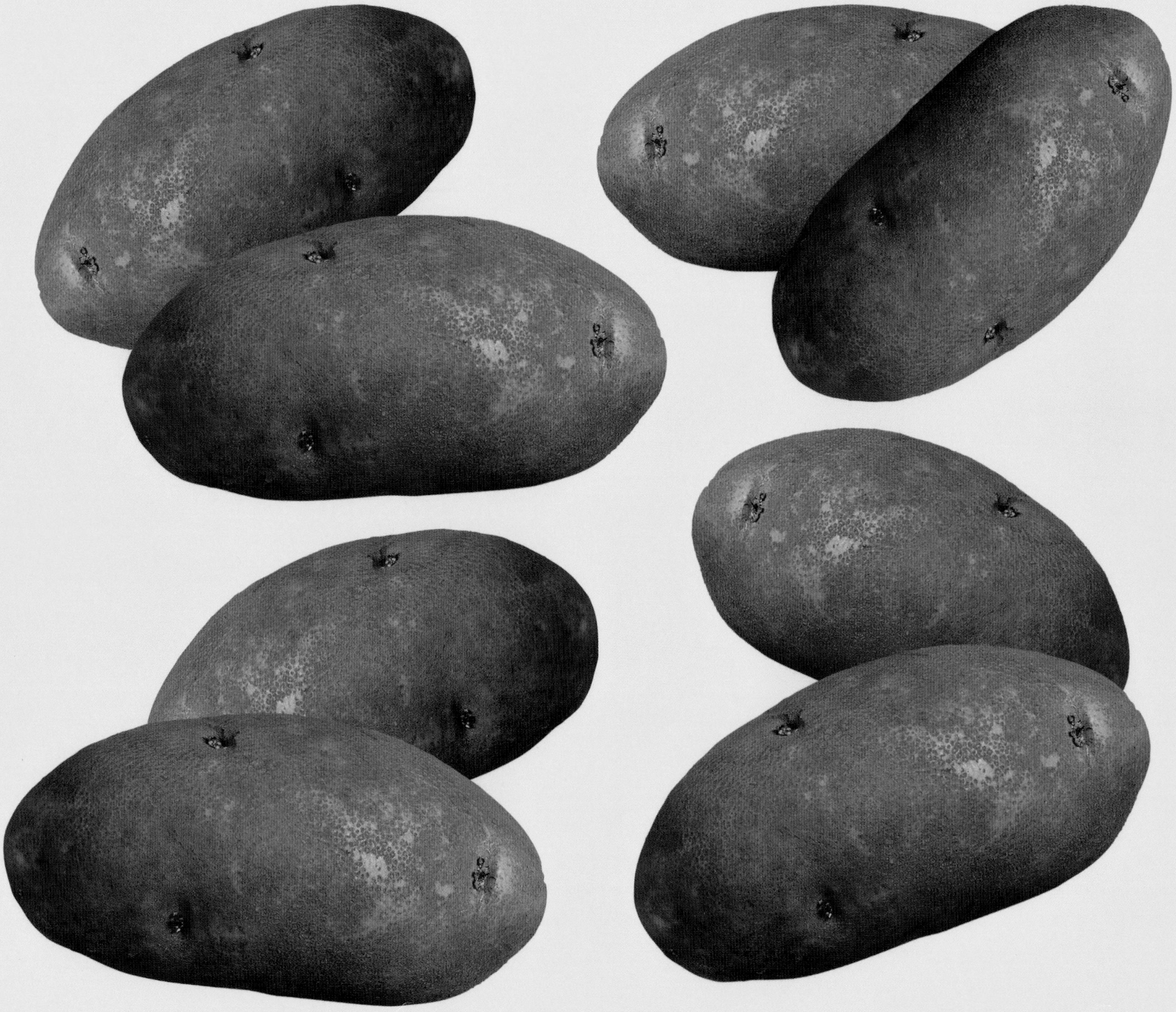

2
4
6
8
10
12
14
16
18
20
100

12

Peaches grow on trees.
This plump fruit makes
a sweet treat. Munch!

Los duraznos crecen en árboles.
Esta fruta sabrosa es un dulce
manjar. ¡Qué rico!

Twelve peaches /
Doce duraznos

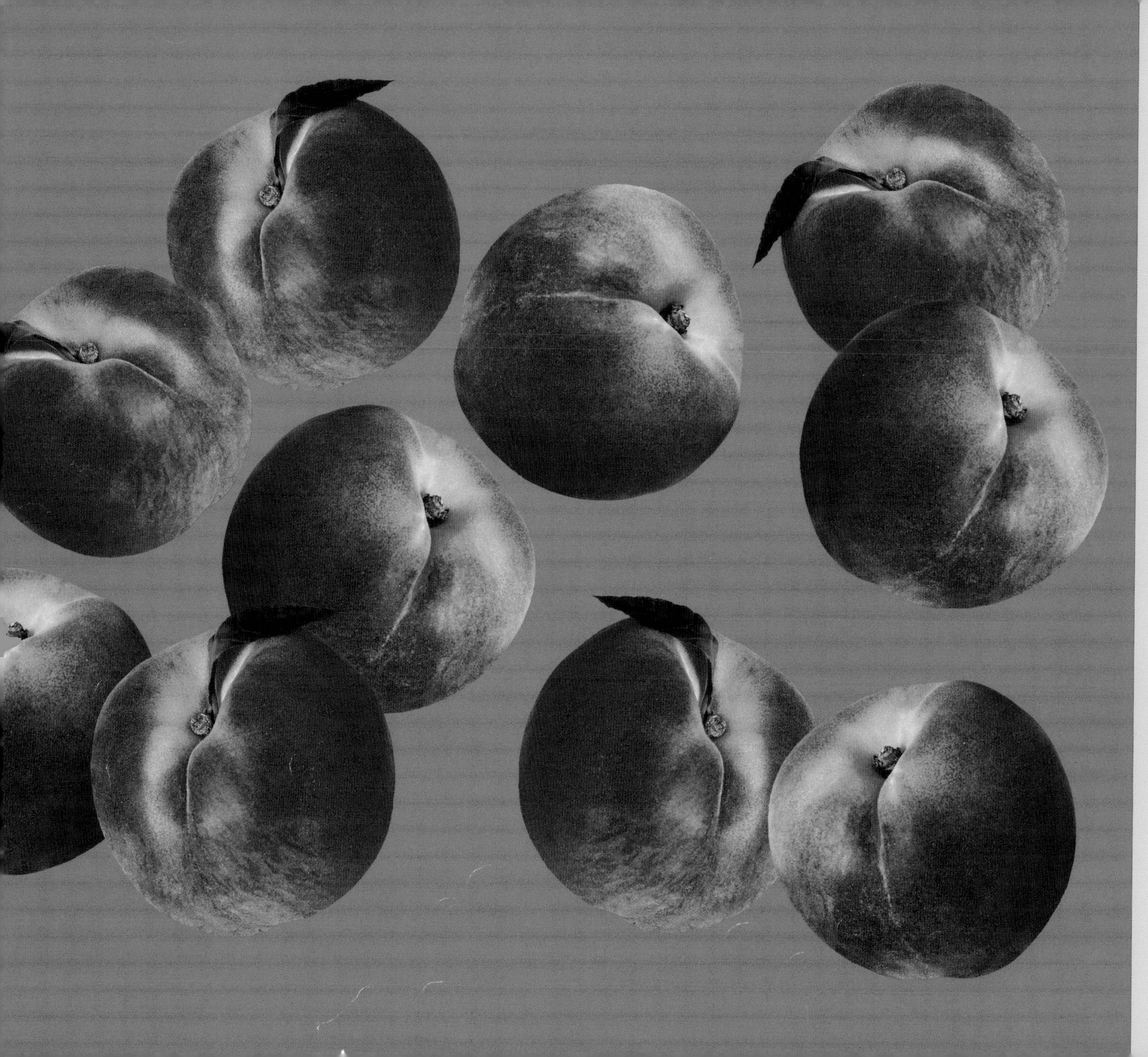

2
4
6
8
10
12
14
16
18
20
100

14

Fourteen raspberries /
Catorce frambuesas

Raspberries come in red, black, or gold. Each berry is a collection of hundreds of tiny fruits, each one containing a seed.

Las frambuesas pueden ser de color rojo, negro o dorado. Cada baya es una colección de cientos de frutas pequeñitas y cada una contiene una semilla.

Sixteen green beans /
Dieciséis habichuelas verdes

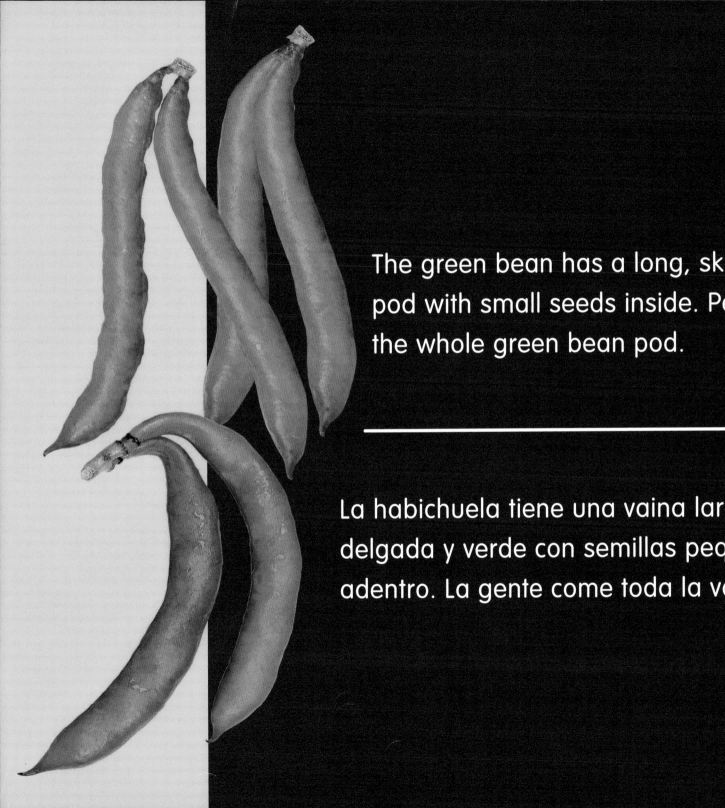

The green bean has a long, skinny green pod with small seeds inside. People eat the whole green bean pod.

———————————

La habichuela tiene una vaina larga, delgada y verde con semillas pequeñas adentro. La gente come toda la vaina entera.

18

Mushrooms are a fungus. People slice mushrooms and eat them on salads and on pizza.

Los champiñones son un hongo. La gente corta champiñones en rodajas y los come en ensaladas y en pizza.

Eighteen mushrooms /
Dieciocho champiñones

20

Twenty tomatoes / Veinte tomates

Many tasty things are made from ripe, red tomatoes. Tomato soup, spaghetti sauce, and ketchup are foods made from tomatoes.

Muchas cosas sabrosas están hechas con tomates rojos y maduros. Sopa de tomate, salsa para espagueti y kétchup son alimentos hechos con tomates.

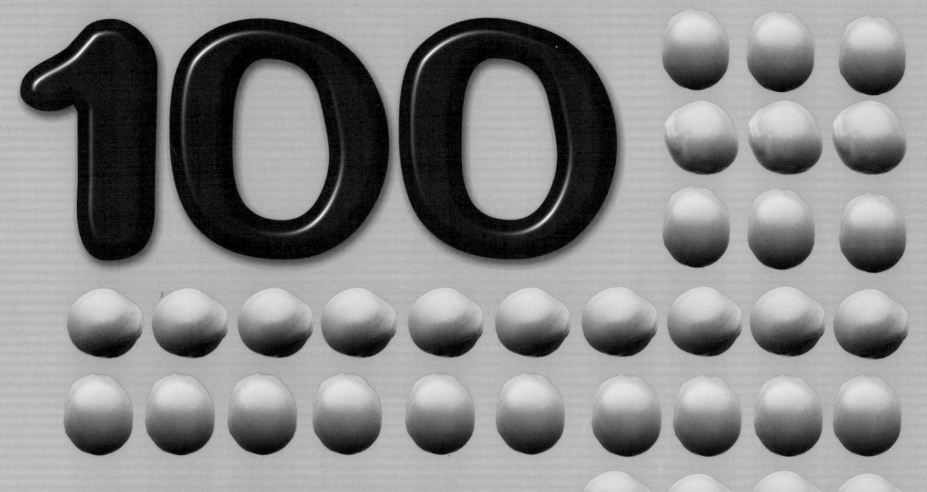

Snow peas and snap peas are green.
Can you count them all?

Los guisantes y los tirabeques
son verdes. ¿Puedes contarlos todos?

24

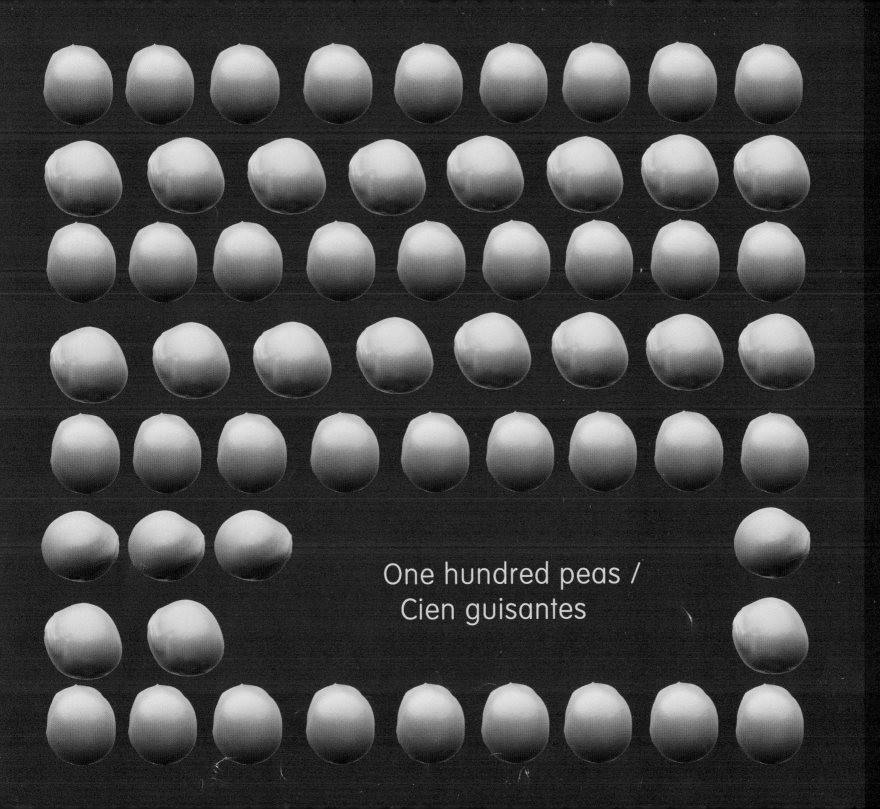

One hundred peas /
Cien guisantes

25

How Many?
¿Cuántos hay?

Tomatoes /
Tomates

Pears /
Peras

Bananas /
Bananas

Raspberries /
Frambuesas

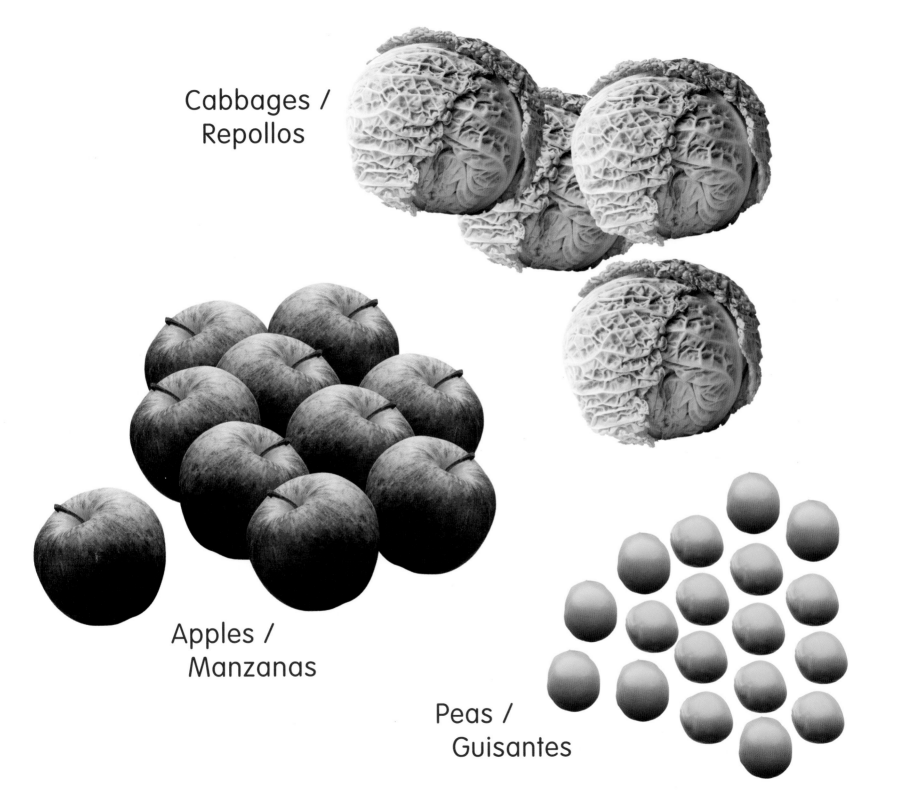

Cabbages /
Repollos

Apples /
Manzanas

Peas /
Guisantes

How do they grow?
¿Dónde crecen?

Apple / Manzana

On trees high above the ground /
En árboles muy arriba de la tierra

Mushrooms / Champiñones

On the ground /
En la tierra

Tomato / Tomate

In gardens close to the ground /
En huertas cerca de la tierra

Raspberries / Frambuesas

On short bushes /
En arbustos bajos

Potato / Papas

Under the ground /
Bajo tierra

Green beans / Habichuelas verdes

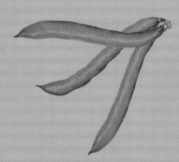

In gardens close to the ground /
En huertas cerca de la tierra

Glossary

fruit—the fleshy, juicy part of a plant that contains one or more seeds

fungus—plants with no leaves, flowers, or roots

seed—the part of a flowering plant that can grow into a new plant; some seeds are hard, but other seeds are soft

tuber—a plant with a thick underground stem

vegetable—a plant grown for food

Internet Sites

FactHound offers a safe, fun way to find Internet sites related to this book. All of the sites on FactHound have been researched by our staff.

Here's all you do:

Visit *www.facthound.com*

Type in this code: 9781429682510

Glosario

la fruta—la parte jugosa y carnosa de una planta que contiene una o más semillas

el hongo—plantas sin hojas, flores ni raíces

la semilla—la parte de una planta floreciente que puede hacer crecer una nueva planta; algunas semillas son duras pero otras semillas son tiernas

el tubérculo—una planta con un tallo grueso bajo tierra

el vegetal—una planta cultivada para comer

Sitios de Internet

FactHound brinda una forma segura y divertida de encontrar sitios de Internet relacionados con este libro. Todos los sitios en FactHound han sido investigados por nuestro personal.

Esto es todo lo que tienes que hacer:

Visita *www.facthound.com*

Ingresa este código: 9781429682510

Index

Check out projects, games and lots more at
www.capstonekids.com

Índice

Hay proyectos, juegos y mucho más en
www.capstonekids.com